GREAT CHORUSES FROM

Great Oratorios

SIXTEEN MIGHTY CHORUSES FROM THE BEST LOVED SACRED
WORKS FOR MIXED VOICES

SELECTED WITH INTRODUCTORY NOTES BY BRIAN KAY

NOVELLO

LONDON

Orchestral material for all the pieces in this volume is available for hire,
as separate items, from the Publisher.

NOV 072517
ISBN 07119-8832-3

Cover illustration: London, Crystal Palace, 1862 from the cover of 'The International
Quadrille' by Charles d'Albert. For the opening day of Crystal Palace 1/5/1862.
Lebrecht Collection
Photograph of Brian Kay © BBC

Published in Great Britain by Novello Publishing Limited
Head office: 14-15 Berners Street, London W1T 3LJ, England
Tel +44 (0)20 7612 7400 Fax +44 (0)20 7612 7546

Sales and Hire: Music Sales Distribution Centre
Newmarket Road, Bury St Edmunds, Suffolk, IP33 3YB
Tel +44 (0)1284 702600 Fax +44 (0)1284 768301

Web: www.musicsales.com e-mail: music@musicsales.co.uk

Music setting by Stave Origination

CONTENTS

BACH	Kyrie from *Mass in B minor*	1
BACH	O man, thy heavy sin from *St Matthew Passion*	17
BACH	Sleep well from *St John Passion*	38
BEETHOVEN	Hallelujah from *Christ on the Mount of Olives*	50
FAURÉ	In Paradisum from *Requiem*	75
HANDEL	Hallelujah from *Messiah*	83
HANDEL	See, the conqu'ring hero from *Judas Maccabaeus*	99
HAYDN	Dona nobis pacem from *Harmoniemesse*	105
HAYDN	Come, gentle Spring from *The Seasons*	125
MENDELSSOHN	He watching over Israel from *Elijah*	137
MENDELSSOHN	Ye nations, offer to the Lord from *Hymn of Praise*	149
MONTEVERDI	Lauda Jerusalem from *Vespers of 1610*	173
MOZART	Lacrimosa from *Requiem*	198
MOZART	Hostias from *Requiem*	203
VIVALDI	Gloria in excelsis Deo from *Gloria*	215
VIVALDI	Et in terra pax hominibus from *Gloria*	224

INTRODUCTION

"Since singing is so good a thing, I wish all men would learne to sing" – so wrote the great sixteenth-century English composer William Byrd, who could have had no idea the extent to which amateur choral singing would become an essential ingredient of our musical life. Although the Victorian heyday of choral societies is currently a thing of the past, when every town or city proudly supported its own choral and orchestral concerts, there is healthy evidence that more and more of us are turning again to singing in choirs, as a foil to our increasingly hectic and computerised lives at the start of the third millennium.

The Choir of the Year competition which takes place in Great Britain every other year produces more singers each time, with well over 12,000 taking part in the year 2000. The televising of the event has changed the way people appear on the platform, with more and more choirs learning their music by heart and indulging in stage presentation that does much to eradicate the potentially fusty image that choral music has sometimes suffered from in the past. It has also meant an increasing sense of adventure in the choice of music and the building of programmes, and the Novello Choral Programme is a major contributor to this process of ever-widening repertoire.

The important thing in my experience with choirs and audiences is to introduce as much variety as possible within the established concert formulae. The 'highlights' culture has also produced a desire among listeners for as widely-mixed a selection as possible and the reason behind this volume – and its companion volumes – is two-fold. It introduces choirs to extracts from some of the greatest works ever composed for choral voices, in the hope of leading on to the complete works. At the same time, it gives choirs an opportunity to use one volume to present a serendipitous selection of choral gems in a single concert, with the hope that it will also lead audiences to investigate further the very special experience and thrill which complete oratorios uniquely offer. Where orchestral parts are required, these are now available for each individual movement included here, without having to hire the complete works. The availability of such a collection as this should hopefully inspire more people to fulfil the wish so fervently expressed by William Byrd five centuries ago.

Brian Kay

Johann Sebastian Bach (1685-1750)
O MAN, THY HEAVY SIN (from *St Matthew Passion*)
SLEEP WELL (from *St John Passion)*
KYRIE ELEISON (from *Mass in B Minor*)

If we consider that the three works by Bach which are represented here are among the greatest of all religious choral and orchestral works – and many believe them to be so – then it is hard to know where to start, in choosing from so rich an array of magnificent choruses. In the two Passions, the role of the choir is to play a major part in the telling of the story – one minute portraying the crowd in a variety of moods, and the next reflecting on the action. The chorus 'O man, thy heavy sin' comes from the end of part one of the *St Matthew Passion* (although it was originally intended as the opening chorus for the *St John Passion*) and in it, the Christian soul bewails the frailty of mankind. It is a supreme example of Bach's genius at embellishing a simple chorale melody, and its considerable demands include very sustained singing of the soprano line. 'Sleep well' comes immediately before the final chorale of the *St John Passion*, and prays for peace and rest for Jesus' soul, as his body is laid in the tomb. In contrast with the relative simplicity of these two movements, the opening Kyrie from the *Mass in B Minor* finds Bach at his most adventurous. Following the great strength of the opening four-bar statement, he then writes the most sublime fugue subject, and gives all five voices the opportunity to relish its grandeur over a very extensive movement. As with so much of Bach's choral music, great stamina is required to do it full justice, building as it gradually does to that glorious moment when this massive structure finally comes to rest on the major chord.

Ludwig van Beethoven (1770-1827)
HALLELUJAH (from *Christ on the Mount of Olives*)

The first of two Hallelujah choruses in this collection comes from Beethoven's only oratorio, which tells the story of the arraigning of Christ on the Mount of Olives. The main role of the chorus is to play the parts of the soldiers and the disciples, but this final movement – a great paean of praise – looks towards the triumph of the resurrection. As this is in the key of C major, Beethoven avoids the particularly high tessitura which makes life so strenuous for the sopranos and tenors in both the *Missa Solemnis* and the Ninth Symphony.

Gabriel Fauré (1845-1924)
IN PARADISUM (from *Requiem*)

Fauré's *Requiem* was written in deeply personal response to the death of his parents, and even though it is the product of a distinguished church musician writing for surroundings with which he was most familiar, it has become one of the most popular works in the concert hall. Although it was composed only a decade or so after Verdi's *Requiem*, the two could hardly be more different. Fauré summed up his thoughts on his own setting: "Somebody called it a lullaby of death", he wrote, "but that's how I feel about death – a happy deliverance, a yearning for the joys of the afterlife, rather than a painful passing away". Nowhere is this 'lullaby of death' more keenly felt than in the closing 'In Paradisum', which has been likened to a vast stained-glass window in sound.

George Frideric Handel (1685-1759)
HALLELUJAH (from *Messiah*)
SEE, THE CONQU'RING HERO COMES (from *Judas Maccabaeus*)

This mighty Hallelujah Chorus is so often heard out of context that it is easy to overlook its immense importance as the climax to part two of Handel's *Messiah*. That second part of the oratorio follows the story of Christ's passion, scourging, crucifixion, death, resurrection, and ascension into heaven and this triumphant chorus celebrates the ultimate victory over sin. On completing this chorus, Handel is reputed to have said: "I did think I did see all heaven before me, and the great God himself". 'See, the conqu'ring hero comes' is another of Handel's best-known choruses – in or out of context – and it forms part of the celebrations which conclude the third part of *Judas Maccabaeus*, as in turn, the youths, the virgins, and the Israelites welcome Judas, victorious in battle. The middle section, for two sopranos, is often sung by solo voices.

Joseph Haydn (1732-1809)
COME, GENTLE SPRING (from *The Seasons*)
DONA NOBIS PACEM (from *Harmoniemesse*)

The two contrasting choruses by Haydn come from major works which he composed towards the end of his life, when he produced a remarkable succession of choral and orchestral masterpieces – *The Creation, The Seasons, The Seven Last Words of Christ on the Cross*, and the final series of great Masses – all within six years. It was after hearing performances of Handel's oratorios during his visits to London that Haydn was inspired to follow such shining examples, and to devote his last years to creating a wealth of glorious choral music. The opening chorus from *The Seasons* – 'Come, gentle spring' – follows the overture, which represents the passage from winter to spring, and in it, there's an opportunity for the upper and lower voices to demonstrate their separate skills, as well as combining, in music of heart-warming lyricism. By contrast, the 'Dona nobis pacem' which ends the last of the six great Masses – the *Harmoniemesse* – is a jubilant conclusion, not only to one of the finest and most uplifting of all Mass settings, but also to Haydn's entire composing life, both soaring to a tremendous climax.

Felix Mendelssohn (1809-1847)
HE WATCHING OVER ISRAEL (from *Elijah*)
YE NATIONS, OFFER TO THE LORD (from *Hymn of Praise*)

Six years separate the two works by Mendelssohn represented here. The so-called
Symphony No 2 (*Hymn of Praise*) was in fact the fourth of his five symphonies to be
completed and in it, he followed Beethoven's example of a choral finale, thereby
creating part symphony and part cantata. The chorus 'Ye nations, offer to the Lord
glory and might' is a fitting conclusion to this choral finale – very much a hymn of
praise on its own. By contrast, the chorus 'He watching over Israel' from *Elijah* finds
Mendelssohn at his most gently reflective, and it comes in the second part of the
oratorio. The prophet is in the wilderness, after asking for his life to be taken away
following his failure to convert the people forever to the one true God. The chorus
quietly encourages faith in the Lord, who lifts us up in times of despair.

Claudio Monteverdi (1567-1643)
LAUDA JERUSALEM (from *1610 Vespers*)

'Lauda Jerusalem' from Monteverdi's *1610 Vespers* is not only the earliest music in this
volume, but also the only selected movement for double chorus. It can be performed
by choirs large or small, so long as they have sufficient numbers to allow equal weight
in all parts, with a particularly strong divided tenor line. The music is based on the
plainsong theme which sounds time and time again (sung mainly by the tenors, with
the sopranos taking over in the Gloria) and round it, Monteverdi weaves the most
intricate writing for the other voices. With a mass of cross-rhythms and some of the
most energetically driven music in the repertoire, it stretches any choir to the limit in
music of this period. The rewards are very great, particularly with the added richness
of Monteverdi's glorious writing for the accompanying instruments – ideally sackbuts,
cornetts, and strings – and, if sufficient space is available, to create antiphonal effects.

Wolfgang Amadeus Mozart (1756-1791)
LACRIMOSA AND HOSTIAS (from *Requiem*)

The mysterious story of the incomplete composition of Mozart's *Requiem* has done
much to increase the fascination audiences have for this work. The quality of much of
its music also accounts for its enormous popularity in the concert hall. The two
movements selected here are the Lacrimosa which ends the Dies Irae sequence and the
prayerful Hostias, which forms part of the Offertorium – almost certainly the last two
sections to be completed by Mozart himself. They both require singing of controlled
beauty and quiet reflection, as well as the ability to explore both ends of the
dynamic range.

Antonio Vivaldi (1678-1741)
GLORIA IN EXCELSIS DEO AND ET IN TERRA PAX (from *Gloria*)

There are several reasons why choirs and concert promoters have made Vivaldi's setting of the Gloria such a regular feature in their programming. One is the economy of its scoring, and the need (in the complete work) for only three soloists. Another is the way in which Vivaldi has written vocal lines that lie very comfortably within the easy range of all four voices in the choir. But beyond that, is the sheer catchiness and relative simplicity of the music itself. These two opening movements contrast the rhythmic excitement of 'Glory to God in the Highest' with the appropriate word-setting of the following section 'And on earth, peace, goodwill towards men', with its long sustained lines and harmonic clashes.

KYRIE

from *Mass in B Minor,* BWV 232

JOHANN SEBASTIAN BACH
edited by Neil Jenkins

Chorus

O MAN, THY HEAVY SIN

from *St. Matthew Passion* (*Passio secundum Mattheum,* BWV 244)

Text by
Sebald Heyden

JOHANN SEBASTIAN BACH
edited in new English version by Neil Jenkins

© 1997 Novello & Company Limited

18

Chorus I,II

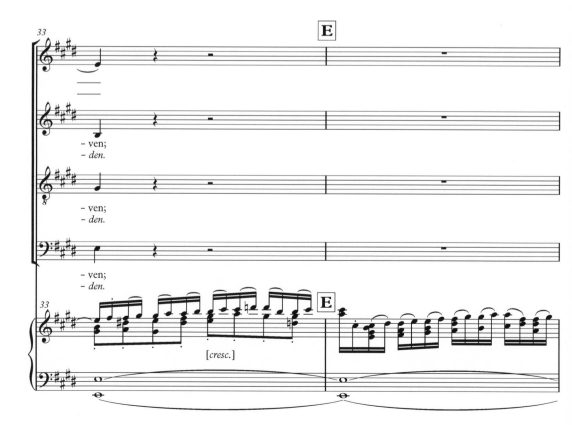

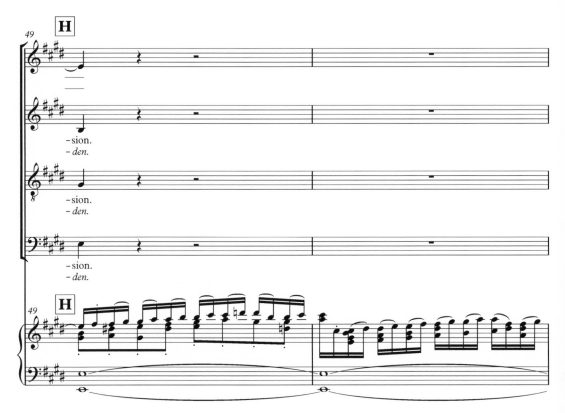

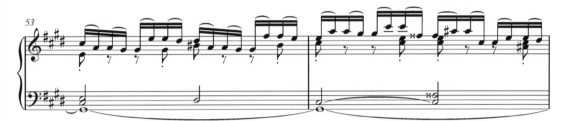

I

(Chorus I,II)

He
Den

He healed the
Den To - ten

sion.
ge.

sion.
ge.

sion.
ge.

SLEEP WELL

from *St John Passion* (*Passio secundum Johannem*, BWV 245)

Text after
Barthold Heinrich Brockes

JOHANN SEBASTIAN BACH
edited in a new English version by Neil Jenkins

61

grave, that was _____ pre - pared _____ for Thee, from ___
Grab, so euch _____ *be - stim* - - - *met ist und* ___

grave, the grave, that was pre - pared _____ for Thee, from
Grab, das Grab, so euch be - stim - *met ist und*

grave, that was pre - pared _____ for Thee, from
Grab, so euch be - stim - - - - *met ist und*

grave, that was pre - pared for Thee, from
Grab, so euch be - stim - *met ist und*

65

all our sor - rows_ sets _____ us free, and points the
fer - ner kei - ne_ Not _____ *um - schließt, macht mir den*

[cresc.]

all our sor - rows_ sets ____ us free, and
fer - ner kei - ne_ Not ____ *um - schließt, macht*

[cresc.]

all our sor-rows sets _____ us free, and
fer - ner kei - ne Not _____ *um - schließt, macht*

[cresc.]

all our sor - rows sets us free, and points the way to
fer - ner kei - ne Not um - schließt, macht mir den Him - mel

[cresc.]

116

Thee, from all our sor - rows_ sets_____ us free, and_
ist und fer - ner kei - ne_ Not_____ um - schließt, macht_

Thee, from all our sor - rows_ sets_____ us free, and
ist und fer - ner kei - ne_ Not_____ um - schließt, macht

Thee,_ from all our_ sor - rows_ sets_ us free,_ and
ist_ und fer - ner_ kei - ne_ Not_ um - schließt,_ macht

points the way to Heav'n, and shuts_____ the gates of Hell. Sleep
mir den Him - mel auf und schließt_____ die Höl - le zu. Ruht

points the way to Heav'n, and shuts_ the_ gates_____ of Hell. Sleep
mir den Him - mel auf und schließt_ die_ Höl - le zu. Ruht

points the way_ to_ Heav'n and shuts the gates of Hell. Sleep
mir den Him - mel_ auf und schließt die Höl - le zu. Ruht

Sleep
Ruht

Dal segno

HALLELUJAH

from *Christ on the Mount of Olives (Christus am Ölberge)*

Text by
Franz Xaver Huber

English Words by
John Troutbeck

LUDWIG VAN BEETHOVEN, Op.85

God's Al - migh - ty Son, Hal - le - lu - jah un - to
-hab' - nen Got - tes - sohn, Wel - ten sin - gen dem er-

God's Al - migh - ty Son. Praise the
-hab' - nen Got - tes - sohn. Prei - set

God's Al - migh - ty Son.
-hab' - nen Got - tes - sohn.

God's Al - migh - ty Son.
-hab' - nen Got - tes - sohn.

God's Al - migh - ty Son.
-hab' - nen Got - tes - sohn.

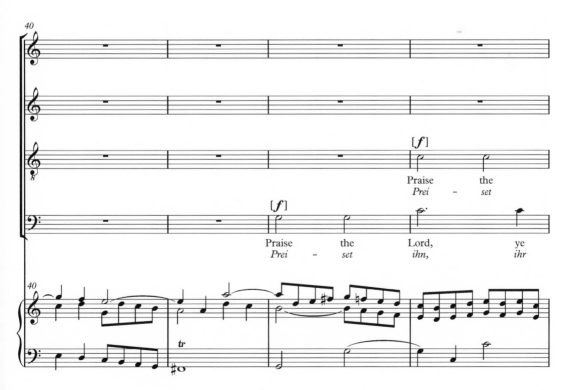

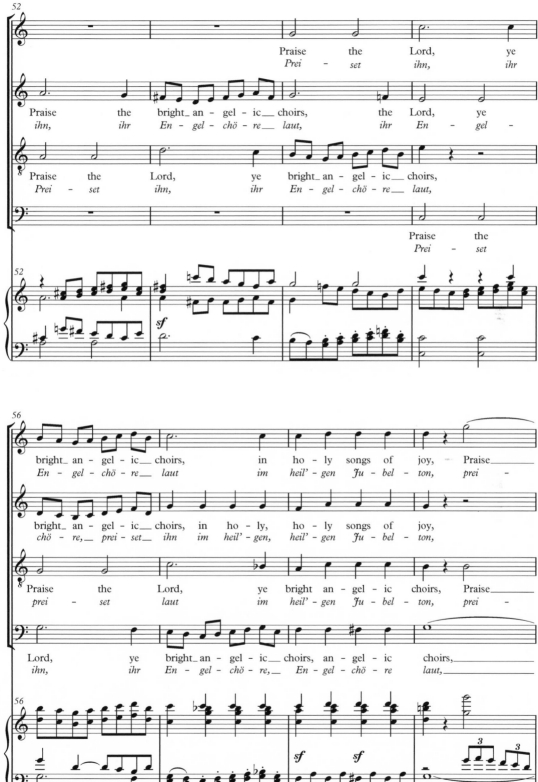

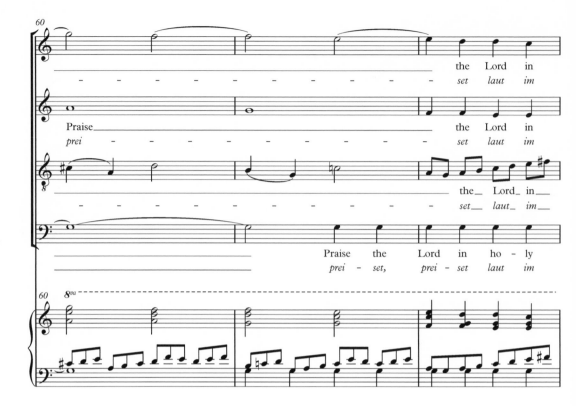

IN PARADISUM

from *Requiem*

GABRIEL FAURÉ, Op.48
edited by Desmond Ratcliffe

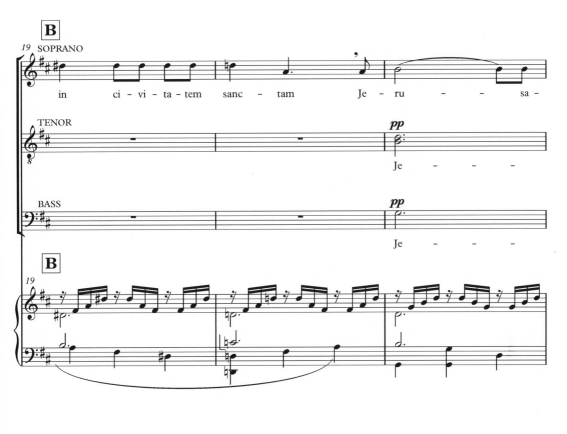

SOPRANO
p sempre dolce

Cho - - - rus An - ge - lo - - rum

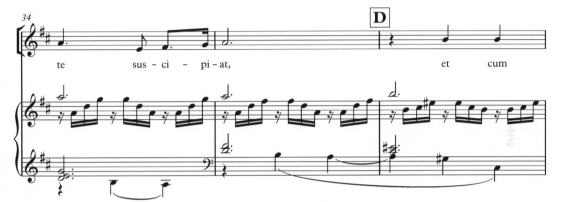

D

te sus - ci - pi - at, et cum

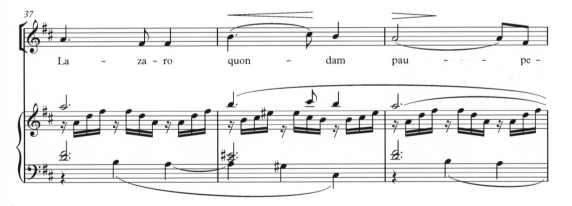

La - za - ro quon - dam pau - pe -

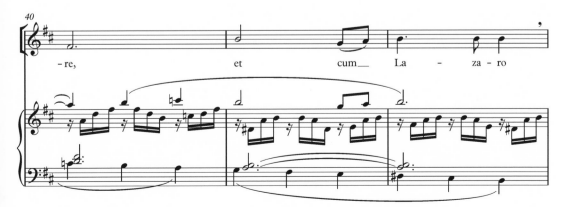

-re, et cum__ La - za - ro

quon - dam___ pau - pe - re æ - ter - nam

SOPRANO

ha - be - as re - - - - - - qui -

ALTO

re - - - qui - - -

TENOR

re - - - qui - - -

BASS

re - - - qui - - -

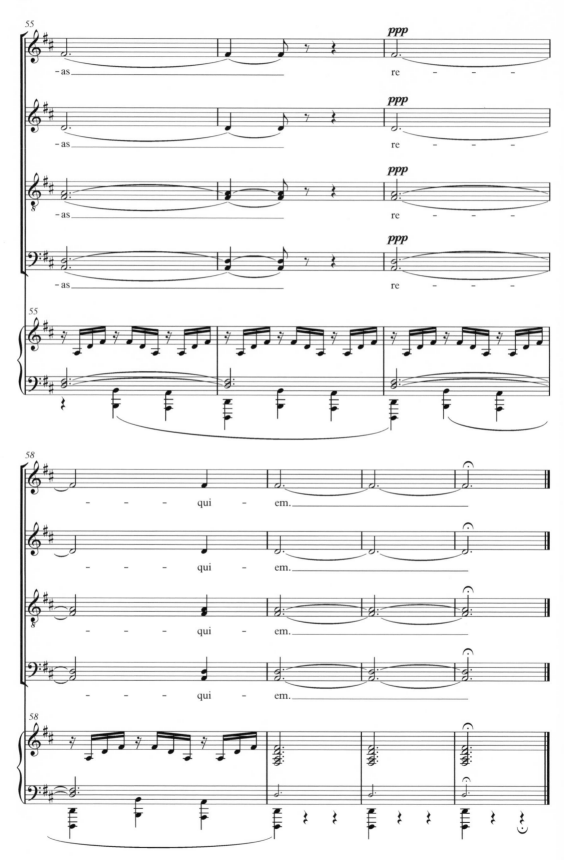

HALLELUJAH

from *Messiah*

Revelation
xix, 6; xi, 15; xix, 16

GEORGE FRIDERIC HANDEL
edited by Watkins Shaw

84

* Alto: Handel himself wrote both notes.

SEE, THE CONQU'RING HERO COMES

from *Judas Maccabaeus*

Text by
Thomas Morrell

GEORGE FRIDERIC HANDEL
edited by Merlin Channon

* The small notes are for rehearsal purposes only.

[segue]

Chorus of Virgins

[segue]

Chorus of Israelites

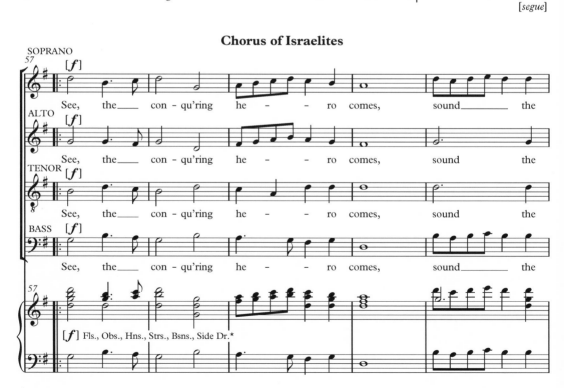

SOPRANO
See, the___ con-qu'ring he - - ro comes, sound_____ the

ALTO
See, the___ con-qu'ring he - - ro comes, sound the

TENOR
See, the___ con-qu'ring he - - ro comes, sound the

BASS
See, the___ con-qu'ring he - - ro comes, sound_____ the

[f] Fls., Obs., Hns., Strs., Bsns., Side Dr.*

* Handel wrote 'Drum ad libitum (i.e. extemporising), the second time warbling (i.e. playing drum rolls).'

trum - pets, beat___ the drums. Sports_____ pre - pare, the

trum - pets, beat___ the drums. Sports_____ pre - pare, the

trum - pets, beat___ the drums. Sports pre - pare, the

trum - pets, beat_____ the drums. Sports pre - pare, the

Senza Side Dr.

lau - - rel bring, songs_____ of tri - umph

lau - - rel bring, songs_____ of tri - umph

lau - - rel bring, songs of tri - umph

lau - - rel bring, songs of tri - umph

DONA NOBIS PACEM

from *Harmoniemesse* (Hob. XXII:14)

JOSEPH HAYDN
edited by Michael Pilkington

* d in original

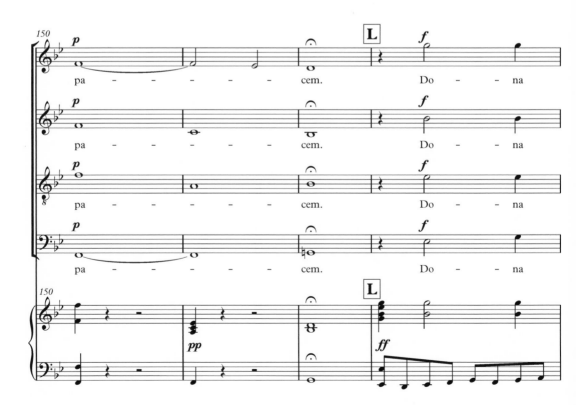

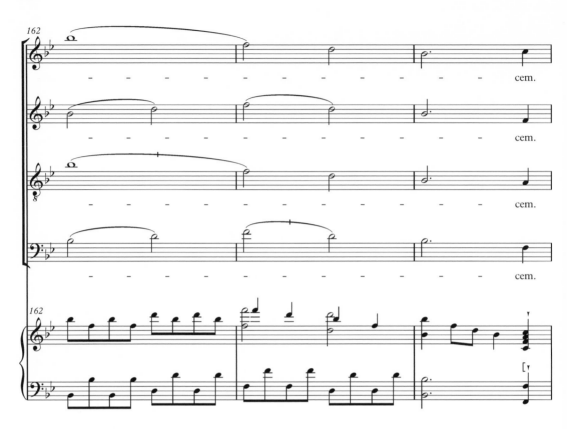

COME, GENTLE SPRING

from *The Seasons* (*Die Jahreszeiten*, Hob. XXI:3)

Text by
Gottfried van Swieten

JOSEPH HAYDN
Edited with a new English translation by Michael Pilkington

breath we feel, and soon will all to life re - turn.
lin - den Hauch, bald le - bet al - les wie - der auf.

breath we feel, and soon will all to life re - turn.
lin - den Hauch, bald le - bet al - les wie - der auf.

And now she nears, and now she nears, the gen - tle
Er na - het sich, er na - het sich, der hol - de

And now she nears, and now she nears, the gen - tle
Er na - het sich, er na - het sich, der hol - de

Spring,_____ and__
Lenz,_____ er__

Spring, and now she nears,_ the gen - tle spring!
Lenz, er na - het sich,_ der hol - de Lenz!

gen - tle spring!
hol - de Lenz!

Spring,_____ and now she nears,_ the gen - tle spring!
Lenz,_____ er na - het sich,_ der hol - de Lenz!

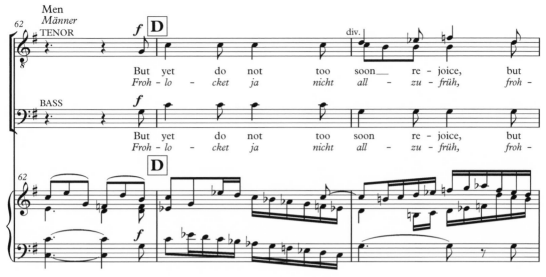

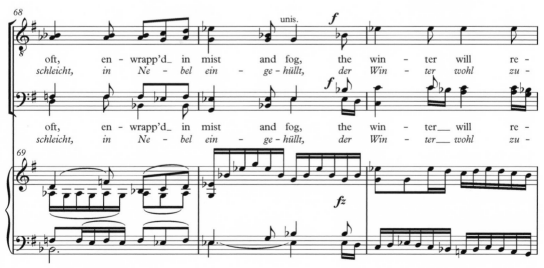

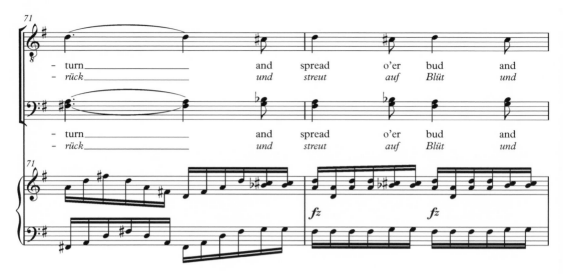

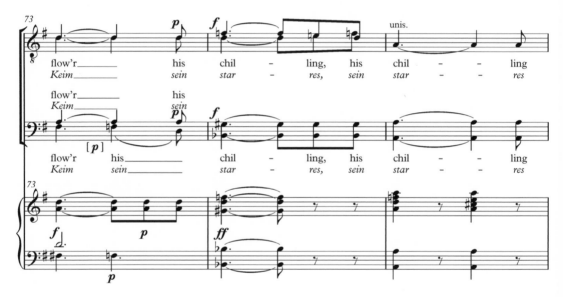

HE, WATCHING OVER ISRAEL

from *Elijah*

Text by
Julius Schubring
after the Lutheran Bible

English version by
William Bartholemew

FELIX MENDELSSOHN, Op.70
edited by Michael Pilkington

YE NATIONS, OFFER TO THE LORD

from *Hymn of Praise (Lobgesang)*

English words
adapted from
Psalm xcvii by
Alfred Novello

FELIX MENDELSSOHN
edited by Michael Pilkington

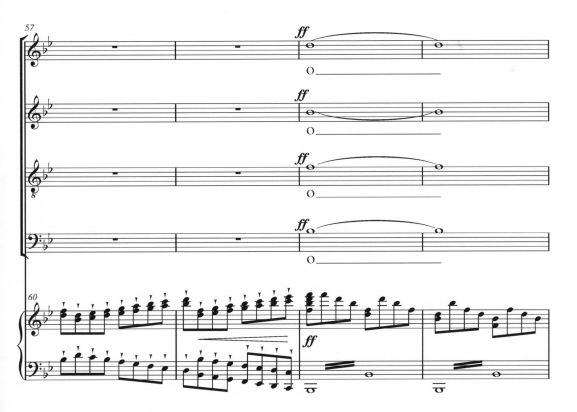

give thanks to the Lord.

give thanks to the Lord.

give thanks to the Lord.

give thanks to the Lord.

LAUDA JERUSALEM

from *Vespers of 1610*

Psalm cxlvii

CLAUDIO MONTEVERDI
edited by Denis Stevens

183

188

190

* Choir I: Strings. Choir II: Fl.1, Ob.2; Bn.1, Tb.1: Bn.2, Tb.3 (Ob.3 and Tb.2 tacet)

Repeat Antiphon on page 173

LACRIMOSA

from *Requiem*, K.626

WOLFGANG AMADEUS MOZART
edited by Duncan Druce

Ju – di-can – dus ho – mo re – us. Hu – ic er – go

Ju – di-can-dus ho – mo re – us. Hu – ic er – go

Ju – di-can – dus ho – mo re – us. Hu – ic er – go

Ju – di – can – dus ho – mo re – us. Hu – ic er – go

par – ce, De – us, Pi – e Je – su,____ Je – su Do – mi-

par – ce, De – us, Pi – e Je – su, Je – su Do – mi-

par – ce, De – us, Pi – e Je – su, Je – su Do – mi-

par – ce, De – us, Pi – e Je – su, Je – su Do – mi-

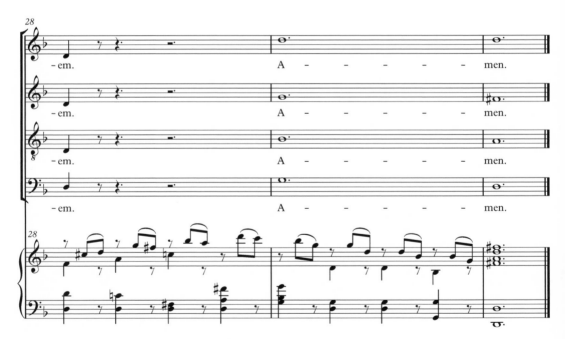

* In bars 24-7 the alto and tenor parts have been altered to provide smoother part-writing. Süssmayr's original reads

On the first beat of bar 25 Süssmayr writes E♭ in the instrumental bass. This has been altered to G to fit the revised choral parts.

HOSTIAS

from *Requiem,* K.626

WOLFGANG AMADEUS MOZART
edited by Duncan Druce

* Süssmayr's tempo indication

ho – di – e, ho – di – e me – mo – ri – am_____ fa – ci – mus.

ho – di – e me – mo – ri – am fa – – – ci – mus.

ho – di – e me – mo – ri – am fa – – – ci – mus.

ho – di – e, ho – di – e me – mo – – ri – am fa – ci – mus.

Fac e – as, Do – mi – ne, de mor –

Fac e – as, Do – mi – ne, de mor – te tran –

Fac e – as, Do – mi – ne, de mor –

Fac e – as, Do – mi – ne, de mor –

GLORIA IN EXCELSIS DEO

from *Gloria*, RV 589

ANTONIO VIVALDI
edited by Jasmin Cameron

ET IN TERRA PAX HOMINIBUS

from *Gloria,* RV 589

ANTONIO VIVALDI
edited by Jasmin Cameron

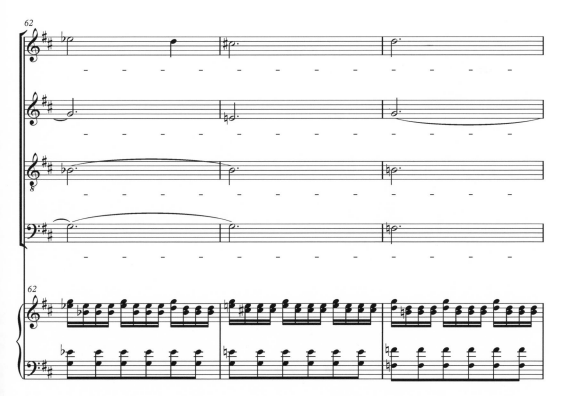

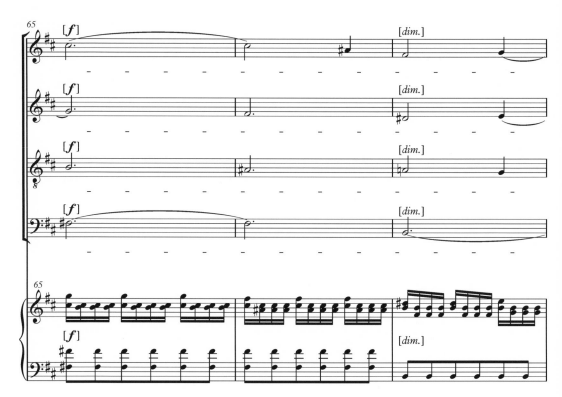

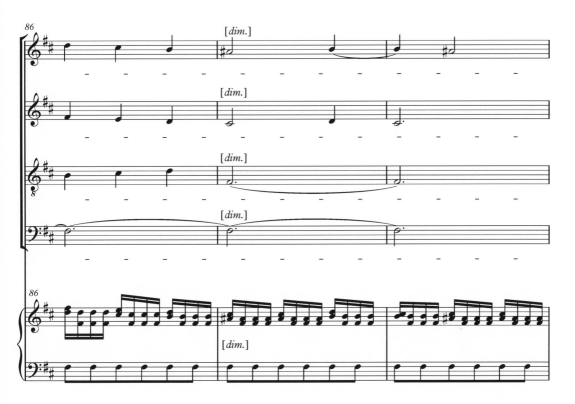